BLAWAT

Great ideas for a port day.
-Mary Martin USA

Even though I only have three days to spend in San Miguel in an upcoming visit, I will use the author's suggestions to guide some of my time there. An easy read - with chapters named to guide me in directions I want to go.
-Robert Catapano, USA

Great insights from a local perspective! Useful information and a very good value!
-Sarah, USA

This series provides an in-depth experience through the eyes of a local. Reading these series will help you to travel the city in with confidence and it'll make your journey a unique one.
-Andrew Teoh, Ipoh, Malaysia

Tourists can get an amazing "insider scoop" about a lot of places from all over the world. While reading, you can feel how much love the writer put in it.
-Vanja Živković, Sremski Karlovci, Serbia

GREATER THAN A TOURIST – UDAIPUR RAJASTHAN INDIA

50 Travel Tips from a Local

Sandra Katarzyna Blawat

BLAWAT

Cover Image: https://pixabay.com/en/udaipur-india-rajasthan-lake-2311788/
https://pixabay.com/en/winter-water-fog-lake-nature-2710049/

Greater Than a Tourist
Visit our website at www.GreaterThanaTourist.com

Lock Haven, PA

ISBN: 9781977003720

>TOURIST

50 TRAVEL TIPS FROM A LOCAL

BLAWAT

BOOK DESCRIPTION

Are you excited about planning your next trip?
Do you want to try something new?
Would you like some guidance from a local?

If you answered yes to any of these questions, then this Greater Than a Tourist book is for you.

Greater Than a Tourist- Udaipur Rajasthan India Sandra Katarzyna Blawat offers the inside scoop on Udaipur. Most travel books tell you how to travel like a tourist. Although there is nothing wrong with that, as part of the Greater Than a Tourist series, this book will give you travel tips from someone who has lived at your next travel destination.

In these pages, you will discover advice that will help you throughout your stay. This book will not tell you exact addresses or store hours but instead will give you excitement and knowledge from a local that you may not find in other smaller print travel books.

Travel like a local. Slow down, stay in one place, and get to know the people and the culture. By the time you finish this book, you will be eager and prepared to travel to your next destination.

BLAWAT

TABLE OF CONTENTS

DEDICATION

This book is dedicated to Samvit Audchiya, the one who made me fall in love with Udaipur and who encouraged me to drink more chai than I could healthily consume.

BLAWAT

ABOUT THE AUTHOR

Sandra is a creative writer and dance facilitator with an education in English Literature, Linguistics and Journalism. After working in the hospitality industry, she decided to call it quits and travel around Asia indefinitely, stumbling into Udaipur as her first stop. The "city of lakes" and all its romantic allure effortlessly convinced her to stay longer than anticipated. Weeks flew by while Sandra propelled herself into work with NGOs and various eco-conscious organizations.

Through these volunteer work trades and extensive time spent with locals, Sandra learned the ins and outs of Udaipur. She would fill her days reading about Rajasthan's history, cooking meals with fresh vegetables from the market and wandering the many lakes and temples familiar to the place.

Though she currently resides on Vancouver Island, Sandra often remembers the red sunsets from atop the hillsides and the reflection of birds dancing in the blue water. Udaipur will always have a space in her heart while she explores her own backyard and continues her work as a writer.

BLAWAT

HOW TO USE THIS BOOK

The Greater Than a Tourist book series was written by someone who has lived in an area for over three months. The goal of this book is to help travelers either dream or experience different locations by providing opinions from a local. The author has made suggestions based on their own experiences. Please do your own research before traveling to the area in case the suggested places are unavailable.

BLAWAT

FROM THE PUBLISHER

Traveling can be one of the most important parts of a person's life. The anticipation and memories that you have are some of the best. As a publisher of the Greater Than a Tourist book series, as well as the popular 50 Things to Know book series, we strive to help you learn about new places, spark your imagination, and inspire you. Wherever you are and whatever you do I wish you safe, fun, and inspiring travel.

Lisa Rusczyk Ed. D.
CZYK Publishing

BLAWAT

OUR STORY

Traveling is a passion of the "Greater than a Tourist" series creator. Lisa studied abroad in college, and for their honeymoon Lisa and her husband toured Europe. During her travels to Malta, an older man tried to give her some advice based on his own experience living on the island since he was a young boy. She was not sure if she should talk to the stranger but was interested in his advice. When traveling to some places she was wary to talk to locals because she was afraid that they weren't being genuine. Through her travels, Lisa learned how much locals had to share with tourists. Lisa created the "Greater Than a Tourist" book series to help connect people with locals. A topic that locals are very passionate about sharing.

BLAWAT

WELCOME TO
> TOURIST

BLAWAT

INTRODUCTION

"Wherever you go becomes a part of you somehow."

- Anita Desai

Udaipur is known as India's romantic city and it sure lives up to its name. In fact, it also goes by: Venice of the East, Blue City, City of Lakes and White City. Each of these carries an accurate portrayal of the town, but there is nothing quite like the feeling of romanticism in the air. A subtle passion that is present in ancient stories, in love and in war and in the environment: palaces, lakes and mountains.

This beautiful city has a rich cultural heritage as it is still inhabited by the Bhil tribe, so expect to see women wearing typical Rajasthani dress with loads of silver jewelry. Though Udaipur has adopted the style of big cities, its customs and traditions remain untouched by the pace of modern times so be mindful of social taboos and manners.

Ultimately, there is an ever-present history here that can only be felt through the senses so enjoy the local cuisine, poetic language and friendliness from the people who echo the rich culture of the Rajputs. After all, the real beauty lies in exploring and experiencing.

BLAWAT

1. Try Poha For Breakfast

Made from beaten rice, poha is cooked easily so many Indians prefer eating it in the morning. Plus, it is a pleasure to watch the street food chef prepare it as quickly as if it were a natural reflex. After frying fennel and mustard seeds, the cook adds onions, turmeric (hence it's dominant yellow colour), salt and some beans. The spices are stirred vigorously then the beaten rice is mixed in with the fried ingredients for a few minutes, until topped off with coriander leaves and a wee bit of lemon. Finally served on a newspaper page.

Despite being cooked in oil, the whole meal is remarkably light and refreshing- though do not be fooled by the small portion (about the size of a palm) because the rice is a filling carb and the spices aren't overwhelming. Much of Indian cuisine is hearty and dense with ghee, coconut milk and chapati, so it's nice to eat something that's easily digestible and won't put you in a food-related coma upon impact.

Wherever you see samosas being fried in the afternoon, expect to see those same men and women preparing poha in the morning. For just over Rs.10 you can enjoy breakfast alongside locals and be energized enough to begin your day.

2. "Unlearn" At Shikshantar Andolan

Shikshantar is an "unlearning space" that confronts conventional educational methods. Manish Jain and his wife Vidhi co-founded Shikshantar: the "People's Institute for Rethinking Education and Development" to challenge existing teaching practises, the current culture of schooling and institutionalized learning.

With these goals in mind, they have created an environment that encourages Indian youth and adults to generate dialogue that critiques models of education while also establishing sustainable, inclusive and horizontal learning structures. Some of their initiatives include: Learning Societies unConference, filmmaking, upcycling workshops (jugaad innovation), Innovations in Shiksha and so on. All directed by the community, for the community.

Every culture and social class is welcome and on Saturdays they host an open house in the form of a "Hulchul" cafe (a communal meal and gift culture). During that time you can wander with curious eyes and speak to members of this grassroots organization. Should you develop an interest in pursuing work with them, they are always happy to accept volunteers with a passion for change.

3. Smile At Strangers

Many travelers find it easy to become intimidated by the faces watching you as you move around town. In the western world, starring is considered rude and in larger cities, eye contact is avoided. In India, however, expect constant attention.

A good approach is to accept the curiosity. After all, you are a foreigner to the locals, thus interesting by default. You will be gawked at, whispered about and sometimes each step you take will be traced on the dusty floors with penetrating eyes.

Just smile back and remain open. It may seem counterintuitive to what you are taught as a child, but smiling and speaking with others can lead to some great friendships especially in Udaipur which is safer than Mumbai or Delhi.

That said, do trust your instincts. If you are alone (and a woman) and feel that smiling could be suggestive, proceed with caution.

4. Rent A Bicycle From Heera Bicycle Store

Cycling in Udaipur is the best way to get a glimpse of the people and the surroundings. In the Lal Ghat area, Heera Cycle Store offers a selection of motorbikes and scooters, or renting a bike for Rs.100-200 for a full day.

You can ride at your own pace and explore the ghats and the local markets. Temple-hopping and rides around the lakes are a common pastime especially in the mornings and evenings before it gets too hot. Or cycle 18 miles through Udaipur villages, see Aravalli hills from close quarters and have breakfast at the deserted Tiger Lake.

Remember to bring your passport as identification and if you are carrying a purse, keep it strapped to you as some people may try to snatch it from you while you ride.

5. Read A Book About The History And Culture of Mewar

Get some background knowledge before entering the plentiful temples and palaces. Mewari is the primary language spoken in Udaipur because it is the historic capital of the kingdom of Mewar, originally Rajputana Agency. The city is therefore steeped in Mewari culture from the food, the buildings and the people.

Many provinces in India vary by customs and traditions because of their distinctive history or environment. Sometimes it feels like one is traveling through a continent connected by countries rather than states. So, it is beneficial to learn about the place you are exploring, why it is different from its neighbors and how it has survived history's trials.

You can find books on Mewar history at Popular Book Store on Bapu Bazar main road.

6. Sleep At Chandra Niwas

This is a homestay where hosts go out of their way to make you feel comfortable and satisfied. Samvit, the son of the small household, is the mastermind behind his family's homestay business. He offers airport pick ups and can even be reached via social media or email before you set foot in the city to help with travel arrangements.

When you arrive at Chandra Niwas, you'll find yourself on a local street without a traveler in sight and facing a charming 3-story building guarded by two St. Bernards. Samvit will then give you a full tour of the kitchen, the two patios and staircases beautified by murals painted by travelers over the years.

The homestay is located outside of the concentrated tourist scene in the downtown core but if you do want to sightsee, Samvit gladly becomes your chauffeur and drives you to the best chai stops, local eateries, or upscale restaurants with magnificent views of Udaipur. As if you have your own personal guide, who happens to be genuinely amicable.

7. Carry Napkins And Hand Sanitizer Everywhere

Indians are culturally conditioned to wash their behinds after using a squat toilet with water from a bucket or a tap. Westerners are not. And although our lavatory experience is not necessarily eco-friendly, we are accustomed to using toilet paper.

In most kiosks you'll find packages of napkins for a couple of rupees. Buy two and always have one on you when walking through a town or village. Do remember to toss it in the garbage pail beside the toilet because the plumbing system in India is not capable of handling paper and feminine hygiene products. That said, if you are a female, it is wise to bring your own menstrual cup or pantiliners as the selection in Udaipur is small.

Coupled with a pack of napkins, hand sanitizer goes a long way. Not just for use after leaving the bathroom, but before and after a meal. There are usually hand washing station at most restaurants, but on the trains and in the street it's advisable to carry the disinfectant. Local cuisine is eaten with your hands, so you want to make sure the dirt you've accumulated from hours of wandering foreign neighbourhoods is gone.

8. Have Chai By Fateh Sagar Lake

Fateh Sagar is a beautiful, artificial lake consisting of tiny islands, one in which holds the Udaipur Solar Observatory. And all around the edges of the lake are chai shops waiting for your service with fresh tea mixed with sugar, milk, ginger and cardamom - at the low cost of ten rupees per cup.

Sipping chai and enjoying the view of the lake is a favourite pastime in Udaipur amongst youth and old men. And on top of a hill bordering the lake is an excellent stall without a tourist around. Here you can watch hoards of men hopping off their motorbikes between daybreak and noon to get their caffeine fix. They nod at one another, catch up on their lives or sit in silence admiring the contrast of cool water in a dry heat.

9. Dance At The Udaipur World Music Festival

Every year in February Udaipur opens its doors to artists from around the globe to give a range of performances, from flamenco to African beats to jazz fusion or Moroccan Saharian soul. Unlike EDM festivals or heavily commercialized stages, this one gives the audience tastes of cultural spirit. Each musical act brings passion and history into their rhythms, hypnotizing the listener with their fresh takes on traditional songs.

The 3-day festival is a unique experience for families, music lovers and a great place to dance. Catch all of it or select an interesting act and head over to that arena as stages are spread all over town.

10. Voyage Into The Sunset On Lake Pichola

The striking Lake Pichola is situated in the middle of downtown, bordered by hundreds of off-white buildings. It can be walked around but the best way to experience its magnificence is to watch the sunset from inside a boat; it's colors shifting from blue in the high sun to golden yellow when its body reflects the sun's last hues.

Boat cruises run from 9am to 6pm with adult admission Rs.300 per hour, children Rs.150 per hour. Taking a cruise around the freshwater lake is the fastest way to reach all angles of the four islands but in the evening, Udaipur's romanticism comes alive through the sparkling water and final rays of sunlight. Nothing more picturesque than the sunset over Jagmandir, emphasizing the surrealistic charisma of this city.

11. Get A Taste Of Rajasthani Cuisine With "Laal Maas"

Laal maas literally translates into "red meat," so it is a non-vegetarian dish made of mutton. A spicy meat curry prepared in a sauce of yoghurt and red Mathania chillies, rich in garlic and served hot so best eaten in the evening. Historically the meal was favoured amongst royalty who consumed game meat that was masked by heavy use of hot spices. Now, it is a popular Rajasthani meal nibbled on with a side of chapati.

Jagat Niwas Rooftop restaurant prepares the traditional dish well and to a spectacular view. Located in Lal Ghat, Chandpole it is a bit difficult finding the place with so many narrow roads so make sure to arrange transport in advance.

12. Learn A Few Phrases

There is a remarkable 780 languages spoken in India, but of those hundreds, Hindi and Mewari are the dominant languages used in Udaipur. Though many of the younger generations speak English, it is the waitresses/waiters, market vendors and transportation officers that often do not. Seeing as you will need to communicate with them, it is recommended to learn a few words.

Many locals in Udaipur who speak Mewari also speak Hindi. Therefore, to make it easier to memorize, here are some Hindi basics:

Hello (formal) - Namaskar
Good / Excellent / Okay / Really? - Accha
How are you - Kya haal hai
Yes - Haan
No - Naa / Nuhi
My name is ____ - Mera naam ____ hai
Do you speak English - Kya aap angrezi bolte hain
I don't understand - Mujhe samajh nahin aata
Please - krpya
Where is the toilet - Shauchaalay kahaan hai
How much does it cost? - Isaka mooly kitana hai?
Thank you - Dhanyavaad
I want to go to - Main jaana chaahata hoon

13. Indulge In Some German Pastries

A German restaurant in India seems like a conundrum. Shouldn't you be enjoying gulab jamun or aloo gobi? Sure. But sometimes you tire of it and feel quite homesick. Besides, Indian sweets are some of the unhealthiest as they're basically fried sugar in huge pots of oil.

Cafe Edelweiss in Udaipur is a refreshing change for those seeking some western comfort food. Whether it's apple crumble, chocolate pie, or sausages and coleslaw, the selection is vast. They also serve cappuccinos, espressos and macchiatos for anyone bored of the usual chai.

Located on Gangaur Ghat with a patio directly in front of Bagore-ki-Haveli, you can people watch while tasting flavour combinations familiar to the western world.

14. Practise Your Photography Skills In Saheliyo Ki Bari Garden

There's a great deal to capture into still life in a city populated with lakes and Saheliyo ki Bari Garden (Courtyard of Maidens) is one such picturesque location. The garden is beautifully constructed with lush green lawns, a lotus pool and marble elephants with a museum in its interior.

The fountains inside are fed by the Fateh Sagar lake so this garden represents an oasis in an otherwise dry Rajasthani landscape. And indeed, it was formerly a retreat for the royal ladies in the 18th Century; for maidens who accompanied the prince.

Photography in the grounds is growing in popularity amid the younger generations so there is no permission required to snap photos, only a Rs.5 fee to enter the exotic garden.

15. Don't Eat Spicy Food The Night Before A Bus Ride

This is often advice you learn from trial and error but hopefully one is wise enough to avoid eating a spicy curry the night before a long journey. Seeing as most of the popular stops outside of Udaipur (Jaipur, Jaisalmer) require a lengthy bus ride, preparing in advance is important.

The buses are surprisingly comfortable, but they do not have washrooms on board and how many times the bus stops for a washroom break is up to the driver. Or the bus may stop in the middle nowhere leaving you to release your bladder in public view.

For such occasions you don't want to spend thirty minutes emptying your bowels because you decided to eat a meal loaded with red chillies. Instead, opt for a moderately spiced meal with a side of chapati to harden your stool. You won't take as many bathrooms trips and when you do, it will be quick and clean.

16. Watch Locals Do Laundry On The Ghats

Udaipur has many opportunities for directionless wandering and shaded benches to sit down. The numerous Ghats along Lake Pichola are perfect for that occasion and they also present a unique experience: watching locals clean their clothes in the water.

From sunrise to noon you'll see groups of women carrying buckets and soap to the steps by the lake. They'll scrub each item with a bar of soap, knead, then pound the item against the antique ground to ensure no dirt is left behind. When each piece has been wrung out, they dip the clothes (or bed sheets) into the water, one by one. Finally, each piece of clothing is laid out flat against the stone floor to dry in the midday heat.

Joining them are men washing their underarms and children playing in the water. The lake is visibly unclean but it seems the population has developed a general resistance to any germs living in the water. As such, they can use a natural resource to complete an arduous chore. A far cry more the private washing machines westerners use to wash their dirty undergarments.

17. Learn About The Carvings On Jagdish Temple

Jagdish temple is one of the most popular tourist sights in Udaipur. Many travelers climb the marble steps into the grounds, but if you spend a few moments closely examining this sacred site, you'll notice the carvings relay mythical messages.

Along the bottom of the outside walls, at the base, is a series of elephants lined in a row, either facing one another or in profile. The next layer up features men riding on horses holding whips, followed by sculpted images of people with instruments, who are socialising or dancing. Occupying the top are carvings of people on pedestals nearly triple the size of the humans below them and posing as though representing a deity.

A local Indian man explained the significance to me: the bottom represents hell (or human suffering) and as the rows increase upward, they are metaphorical symbols of paradise or nirvana. Yet these intricate carvings are only one piece of the whole. The three-storied temple is comprised of hundreds of stone images including Lord Vishnu, Lord Ganesha and Goddess Shakti. Splendid architecture that can occupy the senses for a solid hour.

18. Eat The Meat Out Of A Fresh Coconut

Along the narrow corridors and streets downtown, there are portable stalls selling fresh coconut juice. Here you can purchase a whole coconut with the top sliced open and enjoy the natural juice from a drinking straw.

Make sure to carry a foldable cutlery set so that when you are done sipping the coconut water, you can scoop out the coconut meat. This refreshing treat not only helps with dehydration, but munching on the coconut flesh is a quick appetite suppressor. Just be sure to tell the seller to cut off a big enough opening so you can successfully reach the coconut meat along the shell.

19. Bathe With A Bucket

Only when you're several thousand miles from home do you miss having a shower. Udaipur's luxurious hotels occasionally sport the luxury, however most mid-range hotels and hostels require guests to bathe with a bucket. Let me de-mystify this simple task.

First, be sure to bathe in the morning or afternoon, never in the evening as winter months can be cool in the northern regions. Secondly, if you are in a semi-public area, bring a scarf to wrap around your body so you are not completely naked as it is disrespectful to show your whole body (especially women).

Once you are ready, pour hot water in a bucket, gently dip your hair in and brush the warm water over your body. Then soap up your whole body and repeat with several rinses, using the smaller jug inside the bucket to wash extra shampoo or dirt from your body. It needs to be done hastily because the water does not stay warm long.

Even if you have the option of a shower, choose the bucket wash whenever possible. Environmentally friendly and it puts you in touch with a practice done everyday by Indian families.

33

20. Walk Through The Forest From Kumbhalgarh to Ranakpur

This is a day (or two) long trip outside of Udaipur and not for the faint of heart. But if you're a nature lover and wildlife enthusiast, then this trip is for you.

You will start by getting a taxi in Udaipur to reach Kumbhalgarh at daybreak. When you reach Kumbhalgarh, spend some time walking around the only unconquered fort to date in India, the massive fortified Kumbhalgarh Fort. Once you are ready to begin trekking down contact the forest officer as they have charges and can hire an escort for your 5 mile trip through the temples. The beginning is a descent over large ancient flagstones but beyond the valley the land is fairly flat. The national park is home to wolves, sloth bears, hyenas, jungle cats, wild boars, bulls, leopards and more but it is rather safe as the animals are not interested in human life.

Overall it takes four hours to walk with a local guide through the Wildlife Sanctuary, though you can travel by the narrow, windy road for less time. Likewise, Ranakpur is several hours from Udaipur so you will need to plan your time accordingly.

21. Play Ultimate Frisbee

Aside from cricket, ultimate frisbee is finding its place among sports fanatics and youth in India. Flying Foxes is the first ever ultimate frisbee team in Udaipur and a growing community of energetic youth.

Founded by the vibrant Manish Kataria, the group is comprised of men and women from as young as 16 to as old as 30. All levels are welcome as Manish spends time training players through weekly practise; encouraging individuals to play with passion regardless of skill or professionalism. Subsequently, the camaraderie, feedback and appreciation of each others game is what binds the team together into a family.

For travelers, information about casual practise games and fun learning sessions are posted on the group's social media pages.

22. Buy Local Art

India's surrealistic landscape and sensuous visions are an artists paradise and each handicraft exploring colors with an incredibly vivid imagination. Whether it be embroidery, textiles or other traditional artwork, every piece is an amalgamation of generations of experimentation and a sharp eye for detail.

Visit small villages rather than shopping centres or sit inside an art gallery and you might stumble upon an artist working on a piece. The Tibetan Market, Bapu Bazaar, Hathi Pol Bazaar and countless galleries downtown are great for shopping for artwork.

23. Don't Ride On An Elephant, Do Ride In A Rickshaw

There's a local elephant in town, and only one. Zipping by on a motorbike through the downtown streets and you might catch its towering frame mulling along. Elephants do not have round spinal disks but sharp bony protrusions extending up from their spine which are vulnerable to weight and pressure. This makes it painfully unnatural to have a human body situated on its backside, adding to the discomfort the elephant already experiences living in a concentrated city.

The art village in Udaipur sells rides on this lonely elephant for decent price, but the novelty is not worth the consequence so instead save your money for navigating the streets by rickshaw. They can feel quite as wild as they roar over the ground dodging other vehicles in a speedy disposition.

24. Volunteer With Animal Aid Unlimited

Working at an NGO in Udaipur is easy as there are quite a few; however, not all are credible. Animal Aid Unlimited is a legitimate U.S-based organization that runs a busy animal shelter and hospital.

The place is home to 50 dogs, 20 cows, pigs and donkeys with around 3 acres of land for resident animals to explore. These animals have debilitating diseases that prevent them from returning to the city and many are taken in because they're covered in fleas, ticks and penetrating wounds or with illnesses from consuming plastic. One of the worst being puppies with maggots crawling in open wounds.

Volunteering here you will learn how to treat injuries, how to medicate diseases and how to be comfortable around larger animals. Considering the almost intolerable number of starving cows and stray dogs, it feels good to contribute helping hands in an ongoing crisis.

25. Book Train And Bus Tickets In Advance

If you don't buy a ticket in advance, especially for a train, you could find yourself sprinting through the station at midnight frantically trying to figure out how your booking failed. Then placed in the second sitting class, fighting for seat space the size of an apple.

Booking in advance means either going to the teller and waiting in a long que or finding a reputable travel agent. If you do not know who to trust, speak with your hotel or hostel manager and often they can help arrange transportation for you.

As for buses, it is imperative to buy your ticket in advance because bus drivers can overcharge tourists. Your baggage is included in the price so do not believe the handlers objection that you must pay extra for a bag. Further, make sure to purchase an overnight bus ticket if you are traveling far (to Jaisalmer for example). The buses have private single or double sleeping booths but choose the booths closest to the front so you won't be bouncing up and down from the back tires.

26. Smoke Some Shisha

Nightlife in the city can be scarce. After dinner and a beverage, the palaces light up like twinkling stars but if you happen on rain or tire of wandering, there is also Cafe Rocks for a casual shisha session.

It can be tricky to find so hire a taxi to the restaurant/bar in Ashok Nagar. Located on the top floor, it is a rooftop restaurant though the emphasis isn't always on food. Many groups of young students and old Indian men gather around shisha and beer (and the occasional tequila) to let out their inhibitions. The snacks are mediocre but the cozy ambience and impromptu karaoke under clouds of flavoured smoke is a pleasing alternative to an otherwise sober evening culture.

27. Listen To Sitar And Tabla Above The City

Atop Jagat Niwas Palace Hotel is a restaurant that offers stunning views of the city at night against the backdrop of classical Indian instruments. Sitar and tabla are played by Indian men in traditional dress who dominate the open air with vibrations mimicking the waters below.

The musicians are set up on a white, elevated platform between dining tables, their small stage decorated with flowers and candles, to add a romantic charm to the evening. Though they play throughout the night, the music is never overwhelming, but rather a soothing background piece to the delicious curry plates and stars overhead.

Located in Lal Ghat behind Jagdish temple, make an early reservation at the palace to secure a table that has a panoramic view overlooking the floating Lake Palace. The staff are friendly and accommodating and will ensure your dining experience is nothing short of divine.

28. Folk Show At Bagore Ki Haveli

A great evening activity is the 1-2 hour long show organized daily at Bagore Ki Haveli in Gangaur Ghat. The popular, cultural event focuses on Rajasthani folk dance but also features a ten-minute puppet dance, local music and a magic show.

In some parts of India, tribal dances are used to celebrate the arrival of a child, of changing seasons and for festivals. To have this ancient practise performed at Bagore Ki Haveli, a palace that dates to the 18th century, is to get a glimpse inside Indian culture. Dances include: Mer, Samai, Kalbelia and Banjara.

Tickets are Rs.60 for Indian citizens, and slightly more for tourists. Note a Rs.100 charge for using a camera.

29. Sign Up For A Music Class

Udaipur is an artistic city, so if you are considering learning vocals or drums, why not try your hand at a traditional instrument? Indian music can be difficult to learn, especially sitar, so having an instructor who has devoted his or her entire life to the instrument is helpful.

Classes are available on an hourly basis and most schools found near Lake Pichola. For a culture that is so deeply committed to accessing the soul through the senses, learning music is great way to understand Indian spirituality and to get a taste of history.

30. Rest At The Iconic Taj Lake Palace

One of the most revered hotels in India is the Taj Lake Palace. Situated on an island in the centre of Lake Pichola, it is only accessible by a speed boat and it is an architectural dream. The former palace, now a luxury hotel, is intricately constructed with ornate carvings, glasswork and detailed art on marble. A gorgeous taste of paradise that's hosted generations of royalty including Queen Elizabeth and Jacqueline Kennedy. Each of whom got to stroll around the numerous fountains, gardens and pillared terraces.

Given the appearance of floating on water because of edge-to-edge walls, it also faces east in view of beautiful sunrises. At night, the palace basks in its own shining lights that are mirrored in the water below, directly opposite the enormous City Palace, but with a continual 360-degree view. A true spectacle for those near and far.

The hotel is a pricier sleeping arrangement but included in the steep price are various resources, including: airport shuttle, boat delivery, parking, restaurants, currency exchange, bars and of course a whole range of areas to unwind.

31. Reach Karni Mata ka Mandir By Ropeway

Many people will recommend the Udaipur City Palace as a point of interest, but it requires a hefty entrance fee including camera charges. Instead, you can travel to Karni Mata temple by following the narrow city lanes to Deen Dayal Park. From there, hop on a cable car for Rs.80 and watch Udaipur unfold below you.

Be mindful of closing times to guarantee a way down, and make sure to arrive for the sunset. The adventurous ride up provides a unique vantage point so if you love photography, the glowing lake palace and illuminated town amidst distance mountains are a marvelous sight to behold.

32. Shop For Jootis

If you love colorful Rajasthani art, Hathi Pol Bazaar is an excellent place to begin your search. Now what should you buy? Beyond the huge variety of wooden handicrafts, souvenirs and miniature paintings are the traditional mojdis and jootis.

Essentially slip-on flats, but with hand embroidered mixed sequins, jootis are common footwear. Whereas sandals and shoes require energy to select a proper fit, jootis are usually bought on a whim as they fall apart easily or are too uncomfortable to wear.

But don't let that deter you! Avoid tacky souvenir shops and search for medium-quality jootis (designer stores charge more). They are meant to be snug as the leather is bound to be tough, except the embellished ones. The pearls are tourist bait so ask someone to lead you to where locals shop for shoes. These won't be the fancy kind, but the real, quality kind. A hardy pair is likely to last your whole life.

That said, if you do want vibrant red, purple or blue shoes with rhinestones, they make a great gift and pack small.

33. Watch The Cow Dung

It's no secret that cows roam freely in India, consequently resulting in poop dropped on every square piece of walking space. Sometimes it's flattened down from tires, other times it's fresh, smelly and not a friendly guest on the bottom of your shoe.

Eventually you will be victim to cow dung stuck to your shoes but can do your best to avoid multiple occurrences. Udaipur has impossibly cramped streets downtown and that is where you should be most careful in avoiding stepping on manure. Keep eyes on all sides for feces, and in-coming motorbikes, animals and small children. The cow dung is not so much troublesome as convenient should you be stuck traveling with fowl smelling footwear.

34. Come After The Monsoon

The monsoon spans from July to September and unless you are a fan of unclean streets flooding to your ankles with water, it is better to come immediately after the rain. This is when the whole landscape is rich with greenery and the lakes are at their fullest. If the heat still bothers you, wait until November and stay for Diwali festival. The cooler weather plus twinkling lights on each house adds to your experience.

Udaipur's lakes have dried up before prior to monsoon season, so scratch a springtime trip. Though other parts of India are perfect during Holi and the months beyond, in this city the main attraction is the lakes, and pre-monsoon sees most of them emptier.

35. Eat Thali At Millets of Mewar

Thali is a round platter of various dishes including dal, rice, vegetables, roti, curd and a side of hot peppers. If you want to eat an authentic Rajasthani thali in an health-conscious space, head downtown to Millets of Mewar. There you will have the same ensemble but the roti is made of millet. This grain tastes nuttier, is easily digestible and is alkalizing to the body.

Cooked without oil and with gluten-free, vegan alternatives, the substitute grains are lighter on the stomach; leaving you full but not immobile after your meal.

36. Spend An Afternoon At Shilpgram Arts and Crafts Village

Translated into "Craftsman Village," Shilpgram is a living ethnographic museum showcasing diversities in art, culture and craft between Indian states. At the base of the Aravali Hills, it is comprised of 26 huts in 70 acres of natural surroundings.

Shilpgram Rural Arts and Crafts Complex depicts the aesthetic culture of Rajasthan. There you can shop for antiques, witness traditional song and dance or observe a different way of living. The artisan's village also hosts workshops, a Crafts Bazaar and an open amphitheatre that seats 8000 people.

The best time to visit is during November and December when the annual festival held; however, it is always a great way to spend the day walking around the compound and learning about art that is born from rural villages.

37. Dodge Rats In A Holy Temple

Once you've reached Karni Mata temple, another surprise awaits you inside: rats! Do not be afraid, they do not bite, nor do they carry disease. This is a holy rat temple that sees thousands of freely roaming rats, keeping the white ones in cages as they are representative of the goddess Karni Mata and her sons. Visitors travel near and far to pay their respects to the rodents and some devotees eat, drink and sleep with them as they believe these rats are their ancestors.

Watching rats feast on dead bodies of other rats, or scurrying across the floor in every direction, might make you skittish but it's also endearing. Bring (or buy) some milk and pour it into a bowl. The rats will gather around it and bathe in the same container while giving you an odd sense of pleasure.

But before you leave, make an offering (food) and seek a blessing from Karni Mata, the Hindu goddess that embodies the female warrior spirit. Her followers believe the rats bring luck, success and health.

38. Discover The Countryside With The Responsible Rural Tour

Directly through Chandra Niwas Homestay, one can book a Responsible Rural Tour. This gives you a chance to leave the condensed city and explore unspoiled rural villages; or the "real" Rajasthan. It is an educational tour where you learn about traditional village life, and where you're connected with youth at DAAN Foundation (Development Action Awareness Foundation), a non-profit grassroots organization. There you will discover ongoing rural development projects and engage with children during games and language activities.

The tour is not rushed, and the host/driver provides a generous amount of information, answers questions and is always cracking a new joke. At the end of the day, the tour arrives at a village home where everyone shares dinner prepared by the matriarch in the family. The experience is pleasant and personal because you truly feel a part of the local culture, while far away from any tourism.

39. Join Buskers In Song By Nightfall

During the evenings, Indian families and friends gather around Fateh Sagar lake to play music, gossip or munch on fried snacks. Coming in by motorbike or by foot, the social affair is a nightly rendezvous for all castes.

But it is along the path circling the lake where you will find groups of young musicians playing guitar and singing favourite songs in unison. They take donations but mostly it's a joyous way to pass time between friends, and if you are brave enough to join them, you too can revel in their happiness.

Simply lend a voice or swing your hips and soon they will be celebrating your act of participation, however minor. By dropping yourself into the epicentre of local culture through the universal language of music, you will be surprised how quickly you can establish friendships.

40. Pick Amla Off The Trees

Amla, or Indian gooseberry, is an incredibly sour fruit that grows on medium sized trees in Rajasthan. Round and light green in color, amla is the fruit you want to be eating to fight off bugs or lack of vitamins in your body.

The health benefits of amla are astounding. From increasing metabolic activity to curing sore throats and balancing stomach acid. It's high quantity of antioxidants also repairs skin, hair and the urinary tract while flushing out toxins and acting as body coolant.

Eating amla can ultimately help prevent food borne illness or at the very least keep your digestive tract running smoothly (heavily spiced foods and plentiful carbs are tough on the body if you are not used to them). But before you pick them off a tree, ask for permission as they may belong to a gardener. Or else search for them in any local market.

41. Hire A Motorbike Driver For A Day

Though riding a bicycle throughout town is a popular way to see the city, a motorbike can whip through chaotic traffic quicker, won't dehydrate you from consistent sun exposure and will take you to the outskirts of town where villages, mountains and temples make up the desert landscape.

At a reasonable, well-negotiated rate, a motorbike driver can take the stress off navigating tumultuous roads and plentiful nameless streets. Getting you to your destination safely and in a timely manner.

42. Take Out A Fair Amount Of Cash At The ATM

There is a noticeable lack of banks and ATMs in town and often they are far apart. As such, it is recommended to withdrawal a useful number of rupees, perhaps enough to budget for a weeks worth of spending. This will cut down on bank withdrawal fees and won't leave you helplessly strapped for money when needing to hail a rickshaw or buy food.

Keep the bills in your money belt to prevent theft, and count your expenses daily. Being short of physical cash is equivalent to being broke because unless you are inside a shopping mall, few items are bought using debit or visa cards; and haggling for food cannot be done via digital currency.

43. Stroll Aimlessly Around The White Buildings

Waiting in ques or visiting temples can tire quickly. No matter the grand beauty and ancient history attached to the marvelous structures, sometimes you crave an afternoon spent strolling around without a plan.

Along the banks of Lake Pichola and throughout main streets, white ornamental buildings decorate the scene. Their walls a blank canvas that explores the interplay of color around their edges. Get up close and touch the carvings designed on their bodies or else get lost between alleys connecting them in disjointed patterns.

Udaipur's neighbours called "brown city (Jaisalmer)" or "pink city (Jaipur)" have their own justifications for upholding such titles, so learn about Udaipur's "White City" using your senses. Discover the architecture and neighbourhoods through the smells, colors and sounds.

44. Attend The Baneshwar Fair during a full moon

The Baneshwar fair carries great value for the culture of Udaipur. The word Baneshwar derives from Shiva Linga (Lord Shiva) and means "master of the delta." So, it is primarily a religious gathering with traditional rituals and with more than half the gathering consisting of Bhil tribe of Rajasthan.

Yet thousands of tourists and pilgrims attend the yearly festival in the Dungarpur district, including families from Udaipur (75 miles away). In the month of February on the full moon, the two rivers Som and Mahi meet in Rajasthan which is considered sacred in Indian mythology. The many tribal devotees worship this natural phenomenon in accordance with its mythological symbolism, by submerging themselves in the ash of their relatives and bathing in the river to seeking blessings from Lord Shiva.

There is also a ceremonial aarti held at the temple in the morning and people singing folk songs by fireside in the evening. As well as: traditional dance, acrobatics, animal and magic shows and large Ferris wheels. An exciting and joyous gathering and one that combines spiritual ceremony with fun elements.

45. Wander The Udaipur Solar Observatory

On an island in Fateh Sagar Lake is the Udaipur Solar Observatory (USO). Situated in the cloudless Rajasthani town and surrounded by water, the island provides a favourable atmosphere that makes it the best viewing in Asia. Modeled after the Solar Observatory in California, USO is the primary location to develop solar physics in India.

The observatory is comprised of a large telescope and a "Solar Vector Magnetograph" which determines the magnetic field of the active regions. Sadly tourists are not allowed inside the building as it is rightfully reserved for science, but you are allowed to take a boat across the lake and wander the grounds to get a better image of the place.

46. Find The Treehouse

An oddball activity for the casual adventure-seekers. The treehouse was built in 2000 in a 65 year-old mango tree by businessman Mr. K.P. Singh. Being a passionate and conceptual individual, Mr. Singh nurtured his idea for quite a while, until eventually his genius steered the project forward on a bet that he could maintain property value of a certain area without chopping down its fruit trees.

The 3-story house is supported by this mango tree and though one cannot freely explore the inside without Mr. Singh's consent (it is a private home), you can take photos from the outside. And subsequently marvel at this collaboration using trees as shelter.

47. Watch A Puppet Show at Bharatiya Lok Kala Mandal

Bharatiya Lok Kala Mandal is a cultural institution that studies folk art and culture from Rajasthan, in the hopes of popularizing old art forms. It has a museum that exhibits folk pieces including dresses, puppets, masks and instruments but the most engaging element is the puppet show held regularly in the puppet theatre.

"Kathputli" or "puppets" is an art tradition saturated with history and content. It references Rajasthani ballads and folk tales, while generally performed by local villagers or tribes. The show is an ancient art form, so it is a great way of understanding Rajasthani culture/tradition.

48. Download the 'Let's See India' App Before Your Trip

Let's See India application for your phone or tablet will become a tour guide in your pocket. You can plan your trip by choosing a destination and learning about popular sites or connect with others on the blog.

Features also include: a section that helps plan weekend getaways (day trips), a phrasebook, foods to try, where to shop and the distances to each place from where you're located. Though more of a generic outline of touristy spots, it is great for those who love to organize and plan ahead rather than go by word of mouth.

Easy to use, interactive and free. Available for android and iOS.

49. Witness Classical Beauties That Once Ruled The Road

Car and vintage lovers need look no further than Udaipur's Vintage & Classic Car Collection Museum. Showcasing Cadillacs, Roll-Royce's, Ford Convertibles and other well-preserved rare beauties that are reminiscent of the British rule once present in India.

These cars starred in various movies and television shows, so it is almost as though one is witnessing the fossilized remains of old cinema; all the while gaining insight into the maintenance and upkeep of these old cars.

50. Bring Some Stickers

Udaipur is surrounded by plenty of beautiful villages increasing your chances of exploring their contents. That means there will be young children running around you, curious about who you are and where you come from. Bringing them a piece of home (wherever that may be for you) is a neat way to bridge two cultures together and to offer something else besides words about your home life.

Stickers are a small, fun gift to pack and they do not assume much, other than remaining as a flashy colorful amusement. Children at the schools adore them and if you bring one with the image of a flag from your home country, they will have a lovely memory of your visit.

BLAWAT

TOP REASONS TO BOOK THIS TRIP

FOOD: If you walk into a kitchen while Indian food is being whipped up, you will likely cry from the overbearing scent of chillies and spices being cooked together. This is what makes the dishes irresistible to the palette. Rajasthani cuisine is infused with loads of ginger, spices, chilies, lentils and vegetables that when cooked with ghee or coconut milk and eaten with fresh naan are incredibly tasty.

LAKES: Lake Pichola, Udai Sagar Lake, Fateh Sagar Lake, Rajsamand Lake and Jaisamand Lake are the five prominent lakes of Udaipur. Some are artificial lakes and many house islands with beautiful architecture. But in contrast to the dry desert lands in this state, Udaipur is an oasis.

ART: From Rajasthani dance, to puppet shows, art villages or folk songs, Udaipur has received a rich cultural heritage from bygone years. There is something for everyone whether you are looking for an evening dance performance or are intrigued by the paintings or handicrafts from the tribes residing in and around the city.

BLAWAT

> TOURIST
GREATER THAN A TOURIST

Visit GreaterThanATourist.com:
http://GreaterThanATourist.com

Sign up for the Greater Than a Tourist Newsletter:
http://eepurl.com/cxspyf

Follow us on Facebook:
https://www.facebook.com/GreaterThanATourist

Follow us on Pinterest:
http://pinterest.com/GreaterThanATourist

Follow us on Instagram:
http://Instagram.com/GreaterThanATourist

BLAWAT

> TOURIST
GREATER THAN A TOURIST

Please leave your honest review of this book on Amazon and Goodreads. Thank you. We appreciate your positive and constructive feedback. Thank you.

BLAWAT

NOTES

17312956R00049

Printed in Great Britain
by Amazon